Taking Back the Culture
by Preaching the Kingdom

Roger Dunlop

All Scripture references are from the New International Version Bible unless otherwise noted

ISBN 978–1913446796

Designed and typeset by Derek Johnston

In memory of my sister Jenny

Genesis 5 v 24 KJV

Acknowledgements

Rodney Gamble, Alistair Spence,
Crawford Gribben and Esmond Birnie

Table of Contents

Foreword

In the days of the judges, when every man did what was right in his own eyes, a farmer from Bethlehem was guided by the expectations of God's law and by the promises of his covenant. As the nation descended into anarchy and apostasy, Boaz honoured God's expectations and welcomed those who wished to be God's people – whatever their background. He wasn't called to be a prophet, or a religious leader of any kind. He wasn't called to be a judge, or to begin any kind of "direct action." Nor was he to find common ground with Philistines or Moabites, or to explore whether those cultures had any concept of natural law that could become the basis of a wonderfully diverse and all-inclusive shared Canaanite culture. Instead, Boaz did what he could, where he could – planting and harvesting, accepting responsibilities in his family and in his small town – and, without realising it, played a central part in the unfolding story of redemption that would lead to the birth of Jesus Christ. In his obscurity, in his faithfulness, and in his importance, Boaz might be a good model of the Christian activity that is set out in this book.

For a very long time, Roger Dunlop has been thinking about the lordship of Christ and its relation to everyday life. When I first got to know him, more than twenty years ago, his thinking about these subjects had already led to some significant changes in his career. This book distils what he has learned in his careers in medicine, business, and education, and in his life in family and church, and presents those ideas to his fellow believers as a challenge and as an encouragement.

As our circumstances come ever more to reflect those of the judges, Roger's call to Christian faithfulness becomes ever more acute. Will Christians change the world? In a way, as Roger shows, the answer to that question doesn't matter. For Christians already have changed the world – and, as this book demonstrates, in fields as diverse as medicine, mathematics and music. The challenge for Christians is to recognise that those achievements in culture have come as a consequence of the lordship of Christ. But these are only first–fruits. One day the world will be completely transformed. All the kingdoms of this world will be the kingdoms of our Lord and of his Christ. All things will be made new.

In the meantime, between the achievements of the past and the expectation of the future, Christians should live under Christ's lordship in our homes, schools and employment.

These are the days of the judges. It's our job to plant, harvest, and take up our everyday responsibilities. Jesus Christ will see to the rest.

Crawford Gribben
Professor of History at Queen's University Belfast

Prologue

Shortly before embarking on his momentous but ill–starred voyage on the Pequod with Captain Ahab, Ishmael, as a good Presbyterian, and his heathen companion Queequeg attend the Whaleman's Chapel in New Bedford.

As they wait to hear the sermon on Jonah from the robust and venerable 'Father Mapple' – a sailor and a harpooner in his youth – Ishmael is struck by the pulpit's unusual construction in the manner of the bows of a ship with the Bible on a projecting piece of scroll work and is inspired to note 'the pulpit is earth's foremost part....the pulpit leads the world..... Yes, the world's a ship on its passage out, and not a voyage complete; *and the pulpit is its prow.*'

From Melville's 'Moby Dick'

Introduction

'I write because I don't know what I think until I read what I say' Flannery O'Connor

Why did I want to write this book?

Our culture is changing rapidly – and not for the better! And most Christians and the church generally seem powerless to do anything about it. But we know that in the same way as culture is upstream from politics (and 'culture eats strategy for breakfast'!), so religion and philosophy are upstream from culture. As Henry van Til says; culture is religion externalized. Christians do have a religion – but it does not seem to be having any impact; instead some other 'religion' is taking the initiative. It seems that not only are Christians powerless in this situation – many appear to be quite resigned to being powerless. Christian belief and action, despite many efforts to engage and show their relevance, seems to be almost hermetically sealed off from having any real effect on the culture. How could this be? I have come to believe that this has to do with the understanding many modern evangelicals have about the extent of 'The Kingdom' and the role that the church, its leaders and individual members should play in it; essentially they see the Kingdom they are concerned about as confined to activities inside the church and the hearts of the believers, alongside specific evangelistic efforts.

I am convinced that this approach to the Kingdom (as compared to a full-orbed vision of Christ's dominion over all) is no minor theological issue for scholars to politely discuss, but is a truncated gospel which has led to Christians effectively neglecting or abandoning large swathes of the culture – a strategic error of huge magnitude with catastrophic implications.

The most foundational issue which I briefly aim to address in this book, has been Christ's Kingdom in the world; its basis, its nature and extent, its development and conclusion; and the role Christians have to play in all this. My approach has been to succinctly review and clarify these points, and then to follow through by describing the means whereby they can be practically worked out and the implications of doing so.

Of fundamental importance has been the reality that while modern evangelicalism has retreated from the public square, secular humanism has been all too successful in advancing. In fact there are no neutral matters and secular humanism has taken charge of the public square. Neutrality is a myth; there is a global conflict going on and there is no option to be Switzerland or Sweden.

As I describe in this book, there are several key mechanisms by which Christians can promote and develop Christ's dominion in the culture. These are through the family, through education, through business and through a lifestyle characterized by informed and principled personal decisions. I believe it is crucial that Christians begin to work out Christ's dominion through these pillars of cultural change, and I was keen to play my part in doing so. However, although, like every other Christian, I would have the power to influence through the exercise of my own individual affairs, my personal potential to be effective through the other pillars is somewhat limited.

So, having identified what I felt was the key most pressing priority for Christians today (namely bringing about Christ's dominion and fulfilment of the cultural mandate), and the principal mechanisms for promoting it, I felt frustratingly powerless to contribute much to it personally.

However, on reflection, it remains clear that each of these 3 pillars; the family, education and business (plus other key cultural factors), are subject to an overarching authoritative influence; the sincere preaching of God's powerful word.

This is what the American novelist Melville was saying when he describes the pulpit of the esteemed and famous Father Mapple as indicating that the pulpit leads the world. So the main theme of this book is the power of sincere, God–fearing and Bible believing preaching to transform the whole world and all of human culture.

Therefore, this book is principally directed at those authentic preachers; that they will recognize their responsibility and power in elevating Christ's unabridged dominion and will thereby contribute forcefully to a godly renewal and development of their culture. If I can persuade the reformed and evangelical preachers of today to read this book and to emphasize how Christians can bring about cultural transformation, I will have been able to help effect that change even though I may have had little direct impact through family, business or education.

An important corollary of this core message of Christ's dominion and the power of preaching to effect cultural change through God's people is that this message is positive and optimistic. This is contrary to what has been the prevailing mood among Christians for many years. But with Christ in control ultimate success is certain; there is no question of being 'on the wrong side of history' when Christ is the one who writes the history! Christians should not be passive or merely reactive, when they are the main lever by which Christ is changing the world.

So, why do I want to promote the dominion outlook?

It honours Christ in its core. It will transform the law and culture generally to conform to God's law and honour Christ in the full range of our activities; individual and national. It inspires myself and my fellow believers to joy, optimism and activity. It involves and unites believers in the great, glorious and victorious struggle of the age with everyone having an essential role to play; large or small.

Therefore, although I do not have much personal opportunity to change the culture through family, business or education, and I am not a preacher to preach on those issues to believers, if this book inspires and affects those in the pulpit who have the power to lead the world and change the culture, then I will have been able to play a part in this mighty endeavour.

So, my bold ambition through writing is to serve the King by honouring Christ, manifesting his Kingdom in all its aspects of fullness and diversity and encouraging Christians to be constructive and joyful in the exercise of their essential role in this wonderful enterprise.

And blessing the culture thereby.

Outline Structure

My line of reasoning in this book is reflected in the Chapter structure as shown below;

Chapter One – How most preachers see their role in relation to the culture. Here I describe the prevailing approach to this issue in most reformed churches.

Chapter Two – Why Herman Melville was right. I address here the scriptural and theological basis for my position – challenging the current popular position.

Chapter Three – How the Kingdom has already transformed the world – a review of the extensive achievements that Christ's Kingdom has already obtained.

Chapter Four – Taking back the Culture. Here I describe what can and should be done now by Christians who are committed to making Christ's dominion manifest in the culture.

Chapter Five – Conclusion

Chapter One

How most preachers see their role

The occupants of the pulpits of the modern reformed church do not typically consider that they have any such responsibility or privilege as described by Melville. They see their job as preaching the gospel and motivating, encouraging and equipping their listeners to become more and more fully involved in Christ's Kingdom – which, for them, is essentially synonymous with the life of the Church. Activity outside the 'Box' of the Church is (apart from missionary work) regarded as of little importance, and only of marginal concern to the preacher. Whether such activity be childrearing, caring for elderly or disabled, production of food or other essential manufactured items, or involving law, art, education or a host of other pursuits; the modern Church has little to say about it and even less regard. Obviously, they would recommend that all these occupations are carried out with diligence and integrity, but they are of no lasting or spiritual significance whatsoever. And indeed as these areas and functions are not regarded as being within Christ's true core Kingdom we would have no grounds to expect his strength or assistance in our attempt to carry them out such as Paul might have in mind in Philippians 4 v 13, where he says 'I can do everything through him who gives me strength' or 2 Corinthians 12 v 9–10 where he speaks of Christ's power resting on him. If you get into difficulty carrying out such secular activities, you cannot expect Christ's help; you are on your own – such worldly struggles are not part of the work He is doing in building his Kingdom. And accordingly, your pastor will have little grounds for strengthening or encouraging you. You also need not expect the adversities you may face in your practical life outside the church will provide any benefit to you in enhancing your spiritual growth.

So, the modern reformed pastor sees the Kingdom which he is called to build, and to which his congregation are required to contribute, as confined to the personal spiritual lives of the believers and the activities within the walls of the local church – with the exception of its extension through missionary work.

Essentially, the Kingdom is a spiritual kingdom which is contained within the 'Box' of the Church and the boxes of the congregation's craniums. Indeed, some pastors may well regard it as wrong and spiritually irresponsible for them to waste their efforts in addressing activities wider than these circumscribed areas with their listeners – similar to the apostles' requirement to concentrate on prayer and the ministry of the word in Acts 6.

What, then, are the grounds for the modern church adopting such a relatively truncated version of the Kingdom?

Although those who uphold this prevalent view must surely accept that, in an ultimate sense, Christ is King over all (Matthew 28 v 18) they might, however, say that his wider Kingship is entirely His business – we in the Church have no role whatever in executing or mediating that bigger Kingdom. They would refer to Christ's description before Pilate as His Kingdom being 'not of this world' in John 18 v 36, or that 'the Kingdom of God is within you' in Luke 17 v 21, and would say that there is no warrant for rolling over any of the characteristics of the Old Testament theocracy of Israel into the New Testament Church.

In essence, they would say that there is no scriptural mandate for the

Church to extend its Kingdom involvement to anything beyond the spiritual realm.

The modern church is also essentially pessimistic in its outlook and so would see no hope or potential for such wider activity to produce significant success or benefits. The secular state is regarded as wrong but unconquerable – Satan is seen as the God of this world. So, the church is involved in a prolonged rearguard action as it retreats from secularism's assaults with no sign of any relief apart from Christ's ultimate return; and if God in His Providence decided to deliver such relief it certainly couldn't be expected to be as a result of any action on the Church's part.

In addition, the Church currently is concerned to maintain its openness and acceptability to the wider world so as to make it amenable for unbelievers to come in and hear the Gospel and be saved. By venturing into involvement or public statements on critical issues in too confident or critical a manner it risks alienating itself from those it is trying to reach and also the important arbiters who influence opinion more widely.

Connected with this, however, and more concerning, is the possibility that the Church leaders are like David's brothers when facing Goliath, or the ten spies returned from exploring Canaan; they simply lack the courage or confidence in their God's ability to defeat the secular giant. They are scared that if they try they will only get hurt in the process.

Or perhaps they are only like the servant with the one talent; they have buried their talent of cultural authority for fear of making a mistake in its use.

If, however, the Church were to be interested in developing an impact on the wider Kingdom – how could its influence be mediated?

The principal ways in which the pulpit can promote the wider building of Christ's Kingdom are through the family, through the individual and through education.

The family, for example, is where all education begins, where character is first developed and where the roles in wider culture are begun; individuals extend their personal influence into business, media, arts, law, politics and beyond; and education from primary to postgraduate is where knowledge is accumulated and propagated – all to the glory of God.

Chapter Two

Why Melville was right

'Man by the fall fell at the same time from his state of innocence and from his dominion over nature. Both of these losses, however, can even in this life be in some part repaired; the former by religion and faith, the latter by the arts and sciences' Francis Bacon (1561–1626)

The Cultural Mandate

When God made man in the Garden He had said 'Let us make man in our image, in our likeness, and let them rule over the fish of the sea and the birds of the air, over the livestock, over all the earth, and over all the creatures that move along the ground' (Genesis 1 v 26); and instructed them accordingly; 'God blessed them and said to them, "Be fruitful and increase in number; fill the earth and subdue it. Rule over the fish of the sea and the birds of the air and over every living creature that moves on the ground."' (Genesis 1 v 28).

God had given man dominion over the whole earth and had instructed him to exercise it. The devastating catastrophe of The Fall plunged mankind's future into much turmoil and misery and might have been expected to have erased this dominion calling – but this was not so. After The Fall, and after the further overwhelming judgement of The Flood, Noah is again instructed to 'Be fruitful and increase in number and fill the earth. The fear and dread of you will fall upon all the beasts of the earth and all the birds of the air, upon every creature that moves along the ground, and upon all the fish of the sea; they are given into your hands. Everything that lives and moves will be food for you. Just as I gave you the green plants, I now give you everything.' (Genesis 9 v 1–3).

So, the profound responsibility and privilege of dominion continued and remains with us right up until today, and the promise to Abraham and his descendants that he would be 'heir of the world' (Romans 4 v 13) still stands.

Our successes in exercising this task have been partial and tainted however, and our capacity, within ourselves, for further accomplishments seems utterly inadequate. The description of man in Psalm 8; 'what is man that you are mindful of him, the son of man that you care for him? You made him a little lower than the heavenly beings and crowned him with glory and honour. You made him ruler over the works of your hands; you put everything under his feet: all flocks and herds, and the beasts of the fields, the birds of the air, and the fish of the sea, all that swim the paths of the seas.' seems to be barely recognizable.

But, in Christ, all this is changed.

Christ's Dominion

The dominion of mankind in Adam is unconvincing and uncertain – but what of Christ's dominion?

In Matthew 28 v 18 Jesus tells His disciples; 'All authority in heaven and earth has been given to me.' In this it seems clear that the mantle of earthly dominion originally given in Adam has been assigned to Christ – but what is the background and basis of this revelation?

In Psalm 8 David writes in awe and amazement of God's installation of man in his role over creation;
'You made him ruler over the works of your hands; you put everything under his feet: all flocks and herds, and the beasts of the field, the birds

of the air, and the fish of the sea, all that swim the paths of the seas.' (v 6–8).

This was not primarily a prophecy, but rather a description of the position with which God honoured man at creation. However, as we have already noted, man's dominion and supremacy would have been no more clearly evident in David's time than in ours. Man's authority to rule was crushed and mangled by Adam's devastating failure at the Fall, and all mankind's power and success in this calling has been severely impaired, though not completely eliminated, since then.

The writer of Hebrews addresses this for us (Hebrews 2 v 6–9); he quotes Psalm 8's description of man's position;

'What is man that you are mindful of him, the son of man that you care for him? You made him a little lower than the angels; and crowned him with glory and honour and put everything under his feet.' (v 6–8).

He notes (as we already have above); 'Yet at present we do not see everything subject to him' (v 8) – but continues – 'But we see Jesus, who was made a little lower than the angels, now crowned with glory and honour because he suffered death...' (v 9).

So, although mankind has failed in his execution of his role – it now being beyond his capacity – Christ, the new Adam, has now been elevated to fulfil this position.

This echoes the description provided in Daniel 7 whereby the 'son of man' – the term used by Jesus to describe himself – receives authority from the Ancient of Days;

'In my vision at night I looked, and there before me was one like a son of man, coming with the clouds of heaven. He approached the Ancient of Days and was led into his presence. He was given authority, glory and sovereign power; all peoples, nations and men of every language worshipped him. His dominion is an everlasting dominion that will not pass away, and his kingdom is one that will never be destroyed.' (Daniel 7 v 13–14).

Although Christ's rule over all authorities and powers has been declared and established as we have read in Matthew 28, its execution and manifestation is an ongoing process. This is in line with Christ's own description of the growth of the kingdom in the parables of the mustard seed or the yeast (Matthew 13 v 31–33), and with the description of the kingdom in Daniel 2 whereby the rock that struck and destroyed the earlier kingdoms grew to become a 'huge mountain and filled the whole earth'. It is also of note that the rock makes real tangible contact with the earlier kingdoms – not just through a parallel spiritual world.

This process of developing dominion is seen also in another important passage which refers to Psalm 8's 'you put everything under his feet', namely 1 Corinthians 15 v 24–27;

'Then the end will come, when he hands over the kingdom to God the Father after he has destroyed all dominion, authority and power. For he must reign until he has put all his enemies under his feet. The last enemy to be destroyed is death. For he "has put everything under his feet"'.

This message of Christ as the new Adam restoring in himself the exercise of the creation mandate of dominion intersects through Psalm 8 with another narrative; that of Christ's conquering and destruction of his rebellious enemies.

In the Fall, man not only lost capacity for legitimate dominion over the creation, he also became a rebel against God's authority. We see this in Psalm 2;

'Why do the nations conspire and the peoples plot in vain? The kings of the earth take their stand and the rulers gather together against the LORD and against his Anointed One. "Let us break their chains," they say, "and throw off their fetters."' (v 1–3).

God laughs in response and says to his newly installed King of Zion;

'Ask of me and I will make the nations your inheritance, the ends of the earth your possession. You will rule them with an iron sceptre; and dash them to pieces like pottery.' (v 8–9).

A similar message is provided in Psalm 110;

'The LORD says to my Lord: "Sit at my right hand until I make your enemies a footstool for your feet." The LORD will extend your mighty sceptre from Zion; you will rule in the midst of your enemies.' (v 1–2), and

'The LORD is at your right hand; he will crush kings on the day of his wrath. He will judge nations, heaping up the dead and crushing the rulers of the whole earth.' (v 5–6).

The description in verse 1 of enemies becoming a footstool for Christ's feet refers us again to 1 Corinthians 15 v 27 and Psalm 8 v 6.

But what does this mean for today's church and for individual believers?

The first point to be clear on is that we are 'in Christ'; as attested to in Romans 8 v 1, 1 Corinthians 1 v 30, 2 Corinthians 5 v 17, Ephesians 1 v 13 and in many other places.

Just in the same way that all mankind is 'in Adam' and suffer the consequences of his fall; so all who trust in Christ are born again and are in Him.

Romans 6 makes clear that if we were baptized into Christ we were crucified with and buried with Him and we will also be united with Him in his resurrection. 'In the same way, count yourselves dead to sin but alive to God in Christ Jesus' (Romans 6 v 11).

Not only are we in Christ, but we are His body (1 Corinthians 12 v 27), and this helps us see how we are involved in Christ's exercise of his dominion, as described in Ephesians 1, and with a further reference to Psalm 8;

'...which he exerted in Christ when he raised him from the dead and seated him at his right hand in the heavenly realms, far above all rule and authority, power and dominion, and every title that can be given, not only in the present age but also in the one to come. And God placed all things under his feet and appointed him to be head over everything for the church, which is his body, the fullness of him who fills everything in every way.' (v 20–23)

Christ has dominion over all things and is head of His body, the church; the means whereby He executes His dominion and 'fills everything in every way' is through the church and its individual believers.

So, whereas in Adam our potential for dominion over the world was cripplingly incapacitated by his fall, in Christ – the new Adam – we are empowered again to undertake this privilege and responsibility.

Our exercise of this responsibility is only in Christ, in his power; it will be partial and gradual. As in many long struggles there will be serious failures and setbacks, but the progress will be inexorable towards Christ's final subjugation of all other powers. Each individual's role may be tiny but not unimportant – in the words of Francis Schaeffer there are 'No Little People' (Schaeffer 1974) in this conquest.

As Hans Rookmaaker has said; 'the Christian.... has been made new in Christ...in harmony with God's original intention for man. He has been given the power of God himself by the Holy Spirit, who will help him work out his new life into the world around him' (Rookmaaker 1970).

'So then, no more boasting about men! All things are yours, whether Paul or Apollos or Cephas or the world or life or death or the present or the future – all are yours, and you are of Christ and Christ is of God' (1 Corinthians 3 v 21–23).

Chapter Three

How the Kingdom has already transformed the World

Introduction

'the fact that Jesus Christ died to take upon himself the sin of mankind is not just something for "the soul". The whole cosmos is to be redeemed, to be "bought back", for all things are under the curse of sin and evil. His saving grace.... excludes no aspect of human reality' Hans Rookmaaker

What was the world like when the Holy Spirit descended on the disciples in Jerusalem on the day of Pentecost?

Pax Romana ruled over the 'civilized world'; but it was a brutal and unpredictable environment, harsh slavery was prevalent, women were treated abominably, disease was rife, wars frequent; brutality and violence prevailed.

Outside the margins of the known world life would have been even more unpleasant; paganism would have dominated Europe beyond the Roman Empire, animism in Africa, Buddhism and Hinduism in Asia and the cruelties of the pre–Columbian cultures in Central America. Virtually everywhere the brutality of power was at work.

The world, surely, has been transformed massively for the better since those times but has the Church been involved? Have believers contributed? Given the empowerment of the Holy Spirit delivered at that time, together with Christ's instruction to baptize and make disciples of all nations; has mankind had any more success in fulfilling the cultural mandate and how have the Church and believers mediated the changes?

The first point to note is that Christianity is the world's most numerous

religion, with an estimated 2.19 billion adherents or approximately 28% of the world's population – of course the number of those who can be termed evangelical is much smaller; perhaps 300 million.
Nevertheless, many millions of individuals have become believers and come to individual salvation and transformation – but what about the key components of culture; has the yeast worked through the dough to change the world for the better as described in Matthew 13 v 33?

Henry van Til has written that culture is religion externalized; we will try to look at some of these specific cultural features.

Law
The recognition by law of the intrinsic value of each human being did not exist in ancient times – nor did the right to freedom of conscience, speech, assembly or association. It is wrong to believe that people enjoyed individual rights prior to Christianity; the ancients had not even the idea of what it means.

However, when the Anglo–Saxon and Christian King Alfred the Great compiled his law code in 893 AD he (while drawing on previous Saxon law codes) essentially founded his guidance on the Mosaic law and the Christian principles of ethics, including in particular the principle of mercy. He prefixed his code with Moses' Ten Commandments and, in a paraphrasing of Leviticus 19 v 15, he admonished judges to 'Doom (or judge) very evenly! Do not doom one doom to the rich; another to the poor! Nor doom one doom to your friend; another to your foe!'.
Important implications of this were equality before the law for all, whether rich or poor, innocence unless proven guilty by reliable evidence, and proportionality of punishment.
The 1215 signing of the Magna Carta by King John, which was heavily

influenced by the input of the Church, reinforced these principles including the law of 'habeas corpus'[1] and together provided the foundation for the English system of Common Law. Crucially, under such an approach, the King himself was not above the Law – in the words of the 13th Century English cleric and jurist Henry de Bracton; 'Not under man, but under God and law'. Scottish Presbyterian minister Samuel Rutherford echoed this principle in his 17th Century book 'Lex, Rex' (Law is King). Bracton also elucidated the important principle of necessary intentionality with reference to a crime – criminal intention or 'mens rea'.

This law system was extended through the British Isles; and by British rule and influence throughout its dominions and commonwealth has become the principal legal system dominating the English-speaking world. Notably, this includes the United States where the legal principles outlined above, the Common Law and the significance of the Magna Carta, have also all been foundational to the American system – sharing, as it does, a common root with the English legal system. In testament to this, it was the American Bar Association that erected the Magna Carta monument at Runnymede.

Consequently, these precious principles of equality before the law, presumption of innocence and right to a fair trial, even if often unsatisfactorily applied, have provided – and continue to provide – a substantial bulwark against capricious or tyrannical legal abuses throughout a great part of the modern world. Their roots are in the Bible and its application by legitimate and effective powers and authorities; the consequences of fairness and equality before the Law, and opportunity for redress for the citizens benefiting from such regimes have been immense.

---

1 The legal right of a person to be brought before a court to assess whether his or her detention is lawful

Education

The first universities were founded by the church in the twelfth Century, having sprung out of the cathedral schools. They were devoted exclusively to higher learning, embracing the essential concept of the mutual interrelatedness of all the disciplines, underlain by the assumption of the God who creates and connects everything.

They were not concerned simply with imparting received wisdom, instead their professors were committed to the pursuit and extension of knowledge, and were prepared to criticize the established teachings of the classical writers. Paris and Bologna were the first universities, followed by Oxford and Cambridge, then many others across Europe from Seville to Rostock. They were often very substantial institutions – Paris enrolled 500 students every year, and they were deeply Christian: all of the faculty would have been in holy orders (Stark 2005).

During this period, however, the Church resisted all translations of the Bible into contemporary languages. Perhaps this was to avoid endless and unedifying bickering about its meaning – or more simply, to stifle opportunity for criticism of the teaching or activities of the ecclesiastical establishment. As Charles Spurgeon has said, 'the religion of Jesus makes men think, and to make men think is always dangerous to a despot's power'. Consequently, its readers were limited to those proficient in Latin, Greek or Hebrew. The parishioners' knowledge of the Bible was confined to what their priests told them.

The invention of the printing press by Gutenberg, followed by the translation of the Bible into the vernacular languages in the 16th Century changed all this and engendered widespread denunciation of the Church's doctrines and performance by reformers of various hues. And one conviction shared by the various Protestant movements was that everyone must consult scripture for themselves. This required that they should be able to read.

The consequence of this is demonstrated by the Pilgrim Fathers, who soon after their arrival in Massachusetts, enacted a law that all children must attend school, ensuring that the children should be able to read and write. For townships having more than a hundred households, a school had to be established, 'the master thereof being able to instruct youth so far as they may be fitted for the university'. Similar emphases applied through the other founding states, and throughout Canada, such that by the end of the 18th Century North America had by far the 'most literate population in the world' (Stark 2005). Only sixteen years after landing at Plymouth Rock, the Puritans had founded Harvard, and by the time of the War of Independence there were a total of ten universities (including Yale, Princeton, Columbia and Rutgers) operating in the American colonies – all but one of them having a denominational founding. In England during this period there remained just two universities (Stark 2005).

Similarly, in 1560 after the reformation in Scotland, John Knox outlined a plan in his Book of Discipline to establish parish primary schools in every community for the teaching of the first rudiments of education. This was proposed for its intrinsic worth as well as with the specific purpose that every person should be able to read the Bible for themselves. It was to be implemented in the parishes partly through the Church and partly by state support. High schools were also to be developed for teaching of the Arts and Tongues, and resources for the replenishment of the ancient universities were to be supplied.

The success of this venture, if not complete, was substantial. It made a particular impact on the significant effectiveness of the venerable universities of Glasgow, Edinburgh, Saint Andrews and Aberdeen. These institutions' influence stretched widely through many disciplines – including the academic 'Scottish Enlightenment' – and it has been said that in the eighteenth and nineteenth Centuries Scotland 'made the world'. The effect of Adam Smith's 'Wealth of Nations' alone has been profound and wide reaching.

Indeed, it is only in recent years that the prestige and reputation of Scottish education has declined.

Democracy

'One of the things we were asked to look into was what accounted for the success, in fact, the pre-eminence of the West all over the world, we studied everything we could from the historical, political, economic, and cultural perspective. At first, we thought it was because you had more powerful guns than we had. Then we thought it was because you had the best political system. Next we focused on your economic system. But in the last twenty years, we have realized that the heart of your culture is your religion: Christianity. That is why the west has been so powerful. The Christian moral foundation of social and cultural life was what made possible the emergence of capitalism and then the successful transition to democratic politics. We don't have any doubt about this.' Scholar from Chinese Academy of Social Sciences 2002 (Aikman 2003)

Christian leaders and thinkers have had fundamental and profound involvement in the generation of the underlying principles and subsequent practicalities of modern democracy. These have been propagated and expressed through two great pillars of influence; the United Kingdom and its historic territories and Empire – England rightly being called 'the Mother of Parliaments' and the United States.

From these two great sources democratic concepts have spread to many diverse corners of the world.
It is important to consider how these ideas began and developed so as to become so hugely important in the modern world.

Modern Christian influence on the development of democracy and constitutional politics begins substantially with the thought and writings of Calvin in the early 16th Century. He addressed such fundamental issues as the relationship of church and state, the ultimate source of political authority in society, the role and significance of the lesser magistrate[2] and the political implications of the doctrine of the fall of man.
He believed that the institutions of church and state were two separate spheres of power, both under the authority of God; the state should not control the church – nor should the church be in charge of the secular state.
He considered that the ultimate source of political power in a society resided in 'the whole body of citizens'. Consequently, the king was not above the law, and indeed 'the lesser magistrate' – any person in authority, such as a governor, councillor, or office holder (elected or appointed) under the one in supreme political authority – had the right and duty to restrain and ultimately to depose such a superior who was acting wickedly. In this he was drawing on Roman Catholic conciliar thought whereby a corrupt pope could be constrained, and on the rights of the Electors in the Holy Roman Empire relative to the Emperor. Under this approach it could be considered that an individual is also a lesser magistrate regarding the situations and dilemmas of their own life.
The doctrine of the fall of man, with the corollary that men in power

2 Institutes: IV.XX

will be inclined to abuse their position to the detriment of others, has the implication that the powers required by the state should be separated and balanced to prevent such abuse.

These important views described by Calvin were not greatly expanded by him, but the ideas in them were developed widely by others - firstly by the Huguenots in France and following them by Christian believers in Scotland, the Netherlands, England and colonial and post-colonial America. Their outworking has been profound.

The Huguenots developed a coherent view of religious and political liberties which lent itself to expansion from strictly religious and covenantal application to wider political and constitutional theory.

The most significant points which they addressed were; the limited character of kingly power, the sovereignty of the people and the right to resist tyrants.

They asserted that because man's proper basic state was one of liberty, and the King's right to rule was based on the consent of the people, therefore ultimate authority resided in the people and they, as a whole, were the King's superior. In this understanding the Huguenot Francis Hotman held that 'the king is nothing more than a magistrate for life and is constantly subject to removal by the people for violation of the duties of his office' (Kelly 1992). The duty of government and the king is to protect the liberty and safety of the public and any King who fails in this or abuses his position is a tyrant and an enemy of God and man. In this situation the lesser magistrates have the right to use force against the king.

Such ideas influenced the Dutch in their rebellion against the Spanish in 1568, the constitutional turmoil of seventeenth Century England and the approach of the revolutionary founders of the United States.

In Scotland during the 16th Century the development of implicitly democratic and political ideas by Christian leaders such as John Knox had a strongly covenantal basis. They emphasized the importance of the covenant between God and the people (including the King) under the Law. The King himself was under the law and Knox held that God's covenant with the people gave them the direct right to rebel against ungodly magistrates, whether or not 'lesser magistrates' gave them guidance, and believed that the higher authority of God's word permitted someone of low rank to rebuke another of otherwise higher standing.

Another Scottish Calvinist scholar and writer of the time, George Buchanan, echoing the Huguenots, based the right of revolution on an inherent right of the whole body of the people to elect a ruler and to depose him if necessary, thus laying the foundation for the wider application of this idea outside the Scottish theological context.

They also sought to put into practice Calvin's idea that, under Christ, the Church was a body equal in legal right and standing with the civil state, thereby denying the right of any King or government to rule over the church or grant it legitimacy.

The Calvinistic views on politics and sovereignty articulated by the Huguenots and put into effect in Scotland were to be tested and dramatically expressed in the tumultuous events of seventeenth Century England. At the start of the Century England had a new monarch James I (James VI of Scotland) who was a forceful proponent of the doctrine of the Divine Right of Kings and its authoritarian and uniformitarian implications. His son, Charles I was also committed to this doctrine and enforced his version of high Anglicanism on the English Church to the great displeasure and distress of the Puritans. Given the views regarding the sovereignty of the people and the right to resist tyranny which were already prevalent among the Reformed citizens, resistance to these moves soon became apparent. The first such reaction occurred when he attempted to force Anglican liturgy on the Church of Scotland. Riots began in Edinburgh in 1637, and resistance in Scotland became more robust and determined, eventually resulting in a Covenanting army crossing into Northern England. In an attempt to finance the military defence to this incursion Charles I summoned the Long Parliament in 1640 which, fatefully for Charles, was heavily Puritan in outlook. This led to ongoing conflicts between Parliament and the King and in due course to Civil War, and ultimately the execution of the King in 1649. After the period of the Cromwellian Commonwealth the monarchy was restored in 1660 under Charles II, bringing with it a partial return to divine right rule with control by the King over all aspects of the nation – including the structure and practices of the Church. His brother James II succeeded him upon his death in 1685. He was openly Roman Catholic and declared his intention to force the nation to reconform to Catholicism. This brought him into opposition with the Protestants as a whole, including the Anglicans, and the type of covenantal arguments brought forward by the Huguenots were invoked to justify deposing him in 1688. He was said to have broken the terms of agreement by which he had ascended the throne. He was replaced by his Protestant daughter Mary and her husband William of Orange. However, the terms of the new constitutional settlement of 1689, among many other significant consequences, ensured that the power of the monarchy would thereafter be significantly curtailed and the king's previous absolute power was now transferred to the people – albeit executed by parliament. Therefore the birth of modern representative democracy should be regarded as owing much to the travails of the seventeenth Century in England; through the religious conflicts of that Century and the wars between the Crown and Parliament a relatively stable and effective arrangement was established by the settlement of the 'Glorious Revolution' of 1689.

Calvinistic ideas regarding control of arbitrary rule and the primary source of sovereignty were significantly influential in determining these arrangements which have effectively been the cornerstone of the British Constitution and were foundational to Britain's relative stability and success in the following Centuries.

In the area of North America which was later to become the United States, the early settlers, particularly in New England, were Calvinist Congregationalists. Under the Crown's granting of the various colonial charters the colonists were granted considerable freedom to organize their local government. In arranging their civil government the settlers tended to follow the pattern used for the foundation of their local church congregation, namely on the basis of a covenant between leaders and the people. This approach was a major source for the essentially American style of government with a constitutional structure, under divine law and based on the consent of the people, and entitling them to resist tyranny.

The colonists understood themselves to have the same rights as all Englishmen, including the right to the principle of consent to be governed.

These early settlers also had a commitment to the 'Puritan Hope' whereby they had a desire to reform the entire world – taking possession of the earth. Whereas 'previous theologians had explained the world: for the Puritans the point was to change it' (Kelly 1992). These attitudes clearly also had important implications for how they regarded the significance of a right approach to political structures.

During the eighteenth Century the Protestant population of the colonies was swollen by a huge influx of perhaps 200,000 Ulster–Scots who were predominantly Presbyterians, such that by the time of the Revolution perhaps one sixth of the population was of Ulster–Scots background. Overall about two thirds of the population by then are thought to have had Puritan or Calvinist connections.

The Calvinistic convictions of the revolutionaries based on Knox's teaching of the duty to resist tyranny and the Huguenots' justification of rebellion are apparent in the Declaration of Independence declaring George III to be 'a tyrant... unfit to be the ruler of a free people'. Such an accusation draws a clear parallel with James II who was similarly accused of violating the covenant at the time of the Glorious Revolution of 1688.

Further confirmation of the prevalence of Calvinistic convictions in respect of the danger of man's fallen nature is apparent when it came to the structuring of the constitution of the new Republic whereby there is careful balancing and separation of power among the three branches of the Government; Legislative, Executive and Judiciary.

It is clear, therefore, that through Switzerland, France, Holland, Scotland, England and North America, from the 16th to the 18th Centuries, the Bible-based thinking of Calvinistic thinkers had a profound and beneficial impact on the foundations and practice of Western political structures. The significant principles to which they have given rise are;

- An acknowledgement of the people as a whole as the ultimate source of authority under God
- The idea of the separate spheres of church and state
- The overarching rule of law applying to the governors as much as to the governed
- The right, and duty, of the 'lesser magistrate' and the people as a whole to resist, and, if necessary, depose tyrannical rulers
- The separation and balancing of powers to prevent corrupt exploitation of the people by a single concentrated source of power

And it is these principles which have spread so widely through the particular influence of Britain and the United States.

Science and Technology

'The heavens declare the glory of God; and the firmament sheweth His handiwork.' Psalm 19 v 1 KJV

Despite the technological inventions and developments of China, Islam, India and ancient Greece and Rome, real science only developed once: in Europe.

The pioneers of science believed that the material realm was real, not magical, enchanted, or governed by spirits and demons. They assumed it was understandable because God created it as rational, ordered and regulated by natural laws. People were stewards of creation, who by understanding nature could manage and control it.

The foundations of these ideas about science were in the rejection by medieval Christian scholars of some of the Classical Greek views about the world; such as the idea that the world was eternal and uncreated, or that the Gods were part of the world; subject to its processes – not above or outside it.

They began with Genesis; 'In the beginning God created the heavens and the earth' (Genesis 1 v 1). This told them that the World had a beginning and that the pre–existing God, outside creation, had created it. The first chapter of Genesis also told them that God had made Man in His own image and that He had created him to rule over the rest of the creation; giving Man his dignity, his freedom and his call to dominion over the world.

Man's dignity was further emphasized by the Incarnation – God in Christ coming into the world as a man. Man was important and so was the real world. Jesus Himself was the Truth and in Him were hidden all the treasures of wisdom and knowledge.

These beliefs were the underpinnings of the impetus for a rational and responsible mankind to explore, understand and describe the Creation to the Glory of God.

Scholars continued to pursue these ideas about God, Man and the World – and they pursued them rationally.

But beginning in the 8th Century or earlier, and long before modern science took its full flight in the 16th and 17th Centuries, much marvelous technology had been implemented.

Technology is not simply 'applied science'; whereas science properly consists of organized explanations of nature combined with systematic observation, technology is essentially a practical means of solving problems, and although technology developed in parallel with science, it was not dependent on it and often evidenced more ingenuity and complexity than it. Technological innovations took place in Christian monasteries, whereas science grew in Christian universities.

Aldous Huxley believed that technology developed in the West because, according to the Bible, God commanded human beings to establish their dominion as stewards over the earth (Mangalwadi 2011). This was true, but it was not the only reason that medieval monasteries began to use technology extensively; there were two other significant factors. Firstly, because each moment is a valuable one–time opportunity, they wanted to use technology to ensure that their time was used wisely, and secondly, they distinguished 'work' from 'toil'; to work was to be like God, but toil was part of the curse of sin, and technology could reduce it.

The labour–saving power machines of the later Middle Ages were produced on the implicit assumption of the dignity of mankind and resulted in improvement of the general welfare – reducing drudgery and liberating and empowering the weak and poor.

An example of an early and significant technological device for the harnessing and application of energy for productive work was the water mill. Although apparently available about the same time – the first Century BC – in Jutland, Turkey and China, its first recorded use for grinding grain was in the 6th Century by the abbot Gregory of Tours. Its use became extensive throughout monasteries and other communities in Europe by the 10th and 11th Centuries, including the famous abbey at Clairvaux where there were water-powered machines for milling, tanning and blacksmithing.

From the 12th Century onward windmills were also used extensively, especially in Northern Europe, having been earlier most prominent in Iran and Afghanistan from the 10th Century, from where their use had spread to India, China and into Europe; other technologies also developed and employed widely by these later medievals were wheelbarrows, flywheels, mechanical clocks and eyeglasses.

Why was it that these technologies and subsequent modern scientific endeavour did not take root and expand in the other great cultures such as the Chinese, Indian, Greco–Roman or Islamic?

China should have had science long before Europe, but although the common people may have worshipped an array of small gods, the intellectuals followed 'godless religions' dominated by impersonal, remote 'principles'. Such principles were unable to actually do anything. The Marxist influenced historian Joseph Needham has written that 'It was not that there was no order in Nature for the Chinese, but rather that it was not an order ordained by a rational personal being, and hence... no conviction that rational personal beings would be able to spell out... the divine code of laws which he had decreed...' (Needham 1954–1984). It did not occur to the Chinese that science was possible.

Despite early discoveries in medicine, astronomy and mathematics in India, their religious beliefs about the World as 'Maya' or illusion, or as the dance of God where God and the Universe are one, meant nature has no lawgiver nor 'laws of nature' to be discovered, warranting no grounds for the development of science.

Greek scientific development was stifled by a number of factors; they believed the universe was eternal and uncreated, that there was therefore no conscious Creator – the gods were part of the Universe, and finally that inanimate objects such as the planets were regarded as living creatures or gods. In consequence of the latter the causes of motion of objects could be ascribed to their motives rather than to natural forces. Aristotle, for example, said that celestial bodies move in circles because of their affection for this action. Such views eliminated the impetus for any search for physical theories.

It might have been expected that Islam with Allah as a law-oriented creator god would have had a sound religious basis for the development of science – but for several reasons this did not turn out to be the case. Firstly, Islam assumes that the universe is sustained by Allah's will on a continuing basis, this is based on the Qur'an teaching that Allah does what he pleases. And if what he pleases is variable, then the universe may not necessarily run under consistent laws. This is in contrast to the Christian approach as outlined by Rene Descartes who said that natural laws must exist because God is perfect and 'acts in a manner as constant and immutable as possible', except for the rare occurrence of miracles.

Additionally, upon their contact with Greek learning they adopted its thinking in large part, including fully embracing the Greek concept of the world as a huge, conscious living organism. Many Muslim scholars became committed followers of Aristotle – proclaiming that his physics was complete and infallible.

Thus, classical Greek learning, rather than engendering scientific progress among Christian scholars – who ultimately resisted and rejected it – stifled scientific development in the Islamic world.

The general conclusion is, as Alfred North Whitehead said, the images of gods that these other cultures endorsed were either too impersonal or too irrational to have sustained science (Whitehead 1967).

The scientific perspective which had begun in Europe as an outworking of medieval biblical theology nurtured by the church developed in the 13th and 14th Centuries, but it expanded much more extensively in the 16th and 17th Centuries, when many more people were able to read and study the Bible in their own languages. This passion for science began when the Bible inspired Christians to devote their lives to recovering God's forgotten mandate for humans to take dominion over nature. Thomas Sprat – one of the founders of the Royal Society in 1660 – said that the society's objective was to enable mankind to reestablish 'Dominion over Things' – as in Genesis 1.

At the time of its formation the membership of the Royal Society was overwhelmingly Christian and Puritan. In England at least, the 'Scientific Revolution' was made from the religious motivation of deeply religious people.

But throughout Europe as a whole the great majority of significant early scientific discoveries were made by Christians – the majority of them devout. The historian Rodney Stark has identified the 52 most exceptional scientists of the 16th and 17th Centuries and concluded that all but two were clearly Christian – whether Protestant or Catholic. These people believed that their work was a calling from God and that, since everything exists for the glory of God, it is right for God's people to study all things, including the heavens.

Christian involvement in many of the crucial scientific developments throughout the following Centuries continued with biological classification by Linnaeus, electrical discoveries by Faraday, communication and computer developments by Morse and Babbage. James Joule, Lord Kelvin and James Clerk Maxwell were outstanding in the field of physics – Maxwell was instrumental in initiating the

Latin inscription over the oak door of the famous Cavendish Physics laboratory in Cambridge quoting the words of Psalm 111 v 2; 'The works of the Lord are great, sought out of all them that have pleasure therein' KJV.

There were many, many others – and many who focused on producing technological improvements such as Thomas Newcomen's steam engine, Cyrus McCormick's mechanical reaper and Samuel Morse's telegraph and code; even the pioneers of flight – the Wright Brothers – were Christians.

It might be thought that due to the often asserted 'conflict' between religion and science and the now apparent wide preeminence of secularism, that the great majority of scientists must have abandoned their religious convictions. On the contrary, however, survey studies well into the latter half of the 20th Century have shown that a very high proportion of scientists still adhere to religious views and practice. Christians are still hugely active and significant across the extensive range of areas of scientific endeavour.

During the Middle Ages, many Christians thought that redemption meant a flight from the world, mastery over one's lusts, and a mystical absorption into God. Regrettably, somewhat similar views are also seen within the Evangelical world today, but the serious study of the Bible at the time of the reformation and the scientific impulses which sprang from it, were seeking a restoration of God's likeness, including the recovery of His creative and ordered knowledge of the natural world and power over it.

So, in addition to serving their fellow men through the developments of science and technology, they sought, through controlling and subduing the world, to restore human beings – in Christ – to their original position as God's viceroys on earth.

Mathematics

'*The chief aim of all investigations of the external world should be to discover the rational order and harmony which has been imposed on it by God and which He revealed to us in the language of mathematics*' Johannes Kepler[3]

It is safe to say that many of the great giants of mathematics from the 17th to the 19th Century were Christians, and many were also inspired by the type of understanding of the universe exemplified by the quotation above from Kepler. They were the men who really created modern mathematics. Kepler (1571–1630) succeeded in formulating the mathematical laws of planetary motion. His work was assisted by the work of the Scottish mathematician John Napier in his invention of logarithms – which greatly helped in the development not only of astronomy, but also of dynamics and physics. Napier also invented a multiplication tool known as 'Napier's bones'. In introducing these techniques Napier had been motivated by the desire to relieve the great burden of carrying out complex calculations which mathematics otherwise required. His interests, however, extended beyond mathematics to the realm of theology – where he had written a commentary on Revelation.
Another pioneer who combined interests in both mathematics and theology was Blaise Pascal (1623–1662) from whom the SI unit of pressure is named. He also began by, as a teenager, attempting to assist his tax collector father with his exhaustive and repetitive tax calculations through the invention of a calculating machine (the Pascaline). Known for Pascal's triangle, he made significant work on number theory and probability theory as well as contributions to physics in the areas of hydrodynamics and hydrostatics. His classic theological work; his *Pensées*, although incomplete on his death, had been planned as a comprehensive defence of the Christian faith.

---

3 De Fundamentis Astrologiae Certioribus, Thesis XX

The work done by Pascal (along with Fermat) regarding probabilities was foundational to the subsequent discovery of calculus by Leibniz around 1675. Mathematics was only one of the many fields in which Liebniz showed his talents; law, diplomacy, history, literature and philosophy were all areas to which he contributed, and which combined together to justify his recognition as a universal genius. His two greatest achievements in mathematics were in his invention of calculus and in his contribution to the field of combinatorial analysis. The momentous discovery of calculus embroiled his reputation in a controversy with his towering competitor in this field, Newton, who claimed to have invented it prior to Leibniz. The controversy over who had antecedence in the matter raged on for many years, but it seems likely that both discovered calculus independently at about the same time from slightly different approaches. Leibniz was a Christian and among his widely varied and extensive works he produced writings on theology and Christian apologetics. His contender for preeminence in calculus, Isaac Newton (1642–1727), was one of the truly great pillars of science and mathematics. His involvement in the development of this area of mathematics was only one of his multiple profound discoveries. Among his many scholarly activities he also developed the law of universal gravitation and described the reality of white light as a combination of all the colours. His composition of his masterpiece, Principia Mathematica, is his greatest work; 'the system of the world'. Although adhering to some unusual theological views, Newton too was probably a Christian believer and had a great interest in theological matters. He wrote a number of religious tracts and claimed that all his discoveries had been made in answer to prayer.

The most influential mathematician of the 18th Century was probably Leonhard Euler (1707–1783). He was likely also to have been the most prolific mathematician in history. He was born in Basle in Switzerland

and brought up in a nearby village where his father was the Calvinist pastor. His father initially wanted him to follow him in the pursuit of theology but having had an interest in mathematics himself he had introduced Leonard to the subject and also to members of the Bernoulli family. The Bernoullis were a veritable dynasty of eminent Swiss mathematicians of Huguenot heritage, and advised Leonhard's father of his son's prodigious talents in this area. Realizing that one can serve God through mathematics as well as theology, the father permitted Leonhard to follow his passion for the subject. He worked for most of his life either in Berlin or St. Petersburg and is famous for solving the Seven Bridges of Konigsberg problem[4]. He contributed to the study of topology, graph theory, calculus, combinatorics and complex analysis; he named the square root of minus 1 as i, and was instrumental in the popularization of the use of the Greek letter pi for the calculation of the circumference of a circle. There are many theorems and notations named after him.

Despite his great genius and mathematical prowess he was also talented at communicating his findings in a clear and understandable way, and his success as teacher was contributed to by his total lack of false pride. As the mathematical historian E.T.Bell has described, 'His early religious training influenced him all his life and he never discarded a particle of his Calvinistic faith. Indeed, as he grew older he swung round in a wide orbit toward the calling of his father, conducting family prayers for his whole household and usually finishing off with a sermon.'

A contemporary of Euler was the English Presbyterian minister Thomas Bayes. Although he was interested in the subject of 'Fluxions' his main contribution was concerning his issues of probability leading to the theorem which bears his name. He didn't bother to publicize his theorem during his lifetime, and it was his friend and fellow minister

4 A challenge to devise a walk which would cross each of the city's seven bridges once, but only once. Euler proved definitively that it couldn't be done.

Richard Price who published it after his death.

Bayes theorem is now understood as having a profound range of applications in many areas where probability is important; forecasting weather, identifying forgeries, improving low resolution computer images and identifying email spam. It is said to have been used to crack the Enigma code and to hunt down Russian submarines during the Cold War.

The next great mathematician to be considered is the German Carl Friedrich Gauss (1777–1855). He is known as the Prince of Mathematicians. He came from very humble origins but was a child prodigy - famously at age 10 he was able to solve almost instantaneously a long addition problem which his severe teacher had set the class. He did revolutionary work on functions of complex variables, in geometry, and the convergence of series. Gauss was a Lutheran, he believed that a life worthily spent here is the best, the only, preparation for heaven.

Working around the same time as Gauss was another profoundly influential French mathematician – Augustin–Louis Cauchy. He made pioneering contributions in the fields of mathematical analysis, continuum mechanics and the study of permutation groups in abstract algebra. Cauchy was a committed Catholic and declared Christian – 'I am a Christian, that is to say, I believe in the divinity of Jesus Christ'. He is said to have endeavoured to convert a young William Thompson (Lord Kelvin) – a staunch adherent of the Scottish Free Church – to Catholicism.

Charles Babbage (1791–1871) is referred to as the Father of the Computer; his design for an Analytic Engine – although not constructed during his lifetime - is reckoned to incorporate all the ideas of modern computers. As a young man he had contemplated entering the Anglican ministry, and in later years published a number of works on theology and miracles. Writing in the *Ninth Bridgewater Treatise* he said, 'The object of these pages...is to show that the power and knowledge of the great Creator of matter and mind are unlimited'.

The only Irishman in the panoply of mathematical paragons is Sir William Rowan Hamilton (1805–1865), who has been described as one of the most imaginative mathematicians of the 19th Century. He was the Royal Astronomer of Ireland and worked both in pure mathematics and mathematics for physics, making important contributions in optics, classical mechanics and algebra. He was also a prodigiously talented linguist, and a friend of the poets Wordsworth, Southey and Coleridge. Hamilton was an orthodox and regular member of the Anglican church. Gene Chase has written: 'In Hamilton's Calvinistic theology, as in that of his Scottish friend and pupil Clerk Maxwell, God is the creator both of the universe and the laws governing it.... As a Christian, Hamilton was convinced that the stamp of God is on nature everywhere. He expected a Triune God to leave evidence of the Trinity on everything...'

Overlapping somewhat with Hamilton was another glitteringly brilliant mathematical mind – that of the German Bernard Riemann (1826–1866). He was one of the most original mathematicians of modern times. He died before he was 40, but it is said that he touched nothing without in some way revolutionizing it. His contributions were in the areas of analysis, number theory and differential geometry. He laid the foundations of the mathematics of general relativity; Stephen Hawking has said 'Albert Einstein could not have completed his general theory of relativity had it not been for the geometric ideas of Bernard Riemann' (Hawking 2006). However, he is perhaps most famous for the Riemann Hypothesis – which states: 'All non-trivial zeros of the zeta function have real part one half'. Perhaps the Moby Dick of mathematical research – as described by John Derbyshire in his book 'Prime Obsession' – there is even a prize of one million dollars for a proof or disproof of it.

Riemann was a dedicated Christian, a son of a Lutheran pastor, who saw his life as a mathematician as another way to please God. During his life, he held closely to his Christian faith and considered it to be the most important aspect of his life. He died of Tuberculosis in Italy where his tombstone quotes Romans 8 v 28; 'All things work together for good to them that love God' KJV.

The last mathematician to be considered is John Venn (1834–1923). He was from a long line of distinguished evangelical Venns, and after studying Mathematics at Cambridge he entered the Anglican ministry. However, some years later he returned to Cambridge where he lectured in logic and probability theory. He is famous for Venn diagrams which he introduced in 1880 to represent inclusive and exclusive propositions. Pascal, Leibniz, Newton, Euler, Gauss, Bayes, Babbage, Riemann; the contributions of Christians to mathematics have been truly vital and fundamental, and consequently the development of the whole of mathematics in the last few centuries has been marinated in foundational Christian thinking and approach. Without the influence of Christian believers in this process modern mathematics simply would not exist.

Medicine

The emphasis on caring for the sick, elderly and chronically disabled developed in the early Christian Centuries. This was in contrast to the previously much harsher attitudes. The Graeco–Roman world in which Christianity appeared was often cruel and inhumane. The weak and the sick were despised. Abortion, infanticide and poisoning were widely practised. In the second Century when plague struck the city of Carthage, pagan households threw sufferers out onto the streets, whereas the entire Christian community led by their bishop responded by offering comfort to the victims and taking them into their own homes to be cared for.

In 369 Basil of Caesarea founded the first Christian hospital. It had

300 beds and cared for victims of the plague, had isolation units, wards for sick travellers and a leprosy house. The building of hospitals progressed through the medieval period – Charlemagne decreed that every cathedral should have a school, monastery and hospital attached. Eventually there were few major cities or towns without a hospital, with provision of facilities for the care of leprosy patients being particularly prevalent. Many of these hospitals were run by Benedictine monks – unfortunately in England the suppression of the monasteries by Henry VIII in the 16th Century resulted in many suffering and disabled patients being turned out onto the streets.

A reinvigorated Christian hospital movement began in the 18th Century inspired by the evangelical 'Great Awakening' in Britain and North America. Along with the Christian characteristic of caring for the weak and sick came a renewed and increased awareness of wider social implications and responsibilities. Flowing from this period and onwards many hospitals and other medical institutions were founded and continue to flourish today.

As facilities for the caring for the sick developed so did the medical knowledge for treatment expand. Catholic priest Guido de Cauliaco (1300–1368) wrote the first modern book of surgery, and about this time anatomical dissections began.

It is often said that the Church opposed the introduction of human dissection, but actually there was little resistance to it by ecclesiastical authorities. In fact, human dissection was not permitted in the Greco-Roman world and it was also forbidden by Islam. The Christian universities brought a new outlook. The starting assumption was that what is unique to humans is a soul, not a physiology. Therefore dissections of the human body are not different from studies of animal bodies and have no theological implications. There were benefits to post-mortems in that they might provide evidence of cause of death in suspected murder and they could extend medical knowledge through observation of anatomy.

Dissections had in fact been carried out for two centuries prior to the work of the Flemish anatomist Andreas Vesalius, author of the influential classical anatomy text 'De humani Corporis fabrica libri septem', who remained a devout Catholic in good standing with the Church, from which he had experienced no significant opposition for his work.

Further significant progress towards a modern approach to medicine came from the influence of the 17th Century English physician Thomas Sydenham (1624–1689). He has been called the 'English Hippocrates' and the 'father of English medicine'. He did not accede to the speculative medical theories of the time and was the first to propose the essentially modern syndrome–based classification of diseases. He wrote Observationes Medicae which became a standard textbook of medicine for two centuries. He was the first to describe scarlet fever, explained the nature of hysteria, and promoted the use of laudanum for pain and cinchona bark for Malaria. He is credited with the aphorism Primum non nocere (First, do no harm).

Sydenham was a zealous Puritan who summed up his medical philosophy as follows:

'It becomes every man who purposes to give himself to the care of others, seriously to consider the four following things: First that he must one day give an account to the Supreme Judge of all the lives entrusted to his care. Secondly, that all his skill, and knowledge and energy as they have been given him by God, so they should be exercised for his glory, and the good of mankind, and not for mere gain or ambition. Thirdly, and not more beautifully than truly, let him reflect that he has undertaken the care of no mean creature, for, in order that he may estimate the value, the greatness of the human race, the only begotten Son of God became himself a man, and thus ennoble it with his divine dignity, and far more than this, died to redeem it. And fourthly, that the doctor being himself a mortal man should be diligent and tender in relieving the suffering patients, inasmuch as he himself must one day be a like sufferer.'

An English physician contemporary with Sydenham was Sir Thomas Browne (1605–1682). His book Pseudodoxia Epidemica (Vulgar Errors) was in the vanguard of scientific writing; it challenged and refuted common errors and superstitions of the age and instead promoted the use of reason and the scientific method for the acquisition of understanding. Browne, however, was also a devout Christian who is remembered also for his other major work; Religio Medici (The Religion of a Physician). His style of writing is greatly admired and his contributions had a profound influence on such medical giants as Sir William Osler. Osler himself (1849–1919) is often referred to as 'The Father of Modern Medicine' – he established the medical residency system and emphasized the importance of his students seeing and talking to their patients – 'Listen to the patient, he is telling you what is wrong with him!'

One of those who greatly admired Thomas Sydenham was Herman Boerhaave of Leiden in the Dutch Republic (1668–1738). He is regarded as the founder of clinical teaching and the modern academic hospital and is best known for demonstrating the relation of symptoms to lesions. In his work as a medical educator at the University of Leiden he is credited as developing the system of clinical instruction on which British medical schools are based; he particularly influenced the development of medicine in Scotland – every founding member of the Edinburgh Medical School had studied at Leiden. In his youth Boerhaave had studied for a divinity degree before turning to medicine and remained a devout Christian. A collection of his religious thoughts on medicine were compiled and published as 'Boerhaave's Prayers'.

He is best recalled, however, within the medical fraternity for his description of the eponymous dramatic surgical condition of 'Boerhaave's syndrome' – an acutely ruptured oesophagus.

Christians have also been involved extensively in the practical and scientific developments involved in medicine over many years, thereby contributing to medicine's tremendous success in relieving pain, curing disease and extending lifespans. The profoundly significant principles of vaccination, now used so widely, and ultimately responsible for the elimination of smallpox, were effectively demonstrated by the English physician Edward Jenner (1749–1823). Jenner was a Christian and shortly before his death, stated to a friend; 'I am not surprised that men are not grateful to me; but I wonder that they are not grateful to God for the good which he has made me the instrument of conveying to my fellow creatures.'

Working a little later than Jenner, the French physician Rene Laennec provided another fundamental medical innovation; the stethoscope – and wrote authoritatively concerning its usefulness. Laennec was a devout Catholic, and reputedly a very kind man, – who also advocated objective scientific research; justifying the comment that 'Laennec's life affords a striking instance among others disproving the vulgar error that the pursuit of science is unfavourable to religious faith.'

Another hugely influential Frenchman was Louis Pasteur (1822–1895), famed as the pioneer of germ theory – among many other significant scientific discoveries. Pasteur was also a Catholic and is said to have commented; '...The more I study nature, the more I stand amazed at the work of the Creator. I pray while I am engaged at my work in the laboratory.' One of those influenced by the writings of Pasteur was Joseph Lister (1827–1912). Lister was a Quaker who became Professor of Surgery in Glasgow. He was an accomplished surgeon who made a number of significant contributions to surgical technique and practice, however he is best known, under Pasteur's inspiration, for the introduction of antisepsis during surgery by the use of carbolic acid. As understanding of the germ theory progressed this later developed into the more modern principle of asepsis in surgery. A contemporary of Lister's was James Simpson who was Professor of Obstetrics at the University of Edinburgh who proposed and introduced the groundbreaking use of chloroform for the relief of labour pains. Simpson was a devout adherent of the Free Church of Scotland; he made a number of other major contributions to obstetric practice – but it is for the introduction of chloroform that he is most famous.

Described above are only a few of those who have made noteworthy impacts upon medical practice from a Christian perspective – there are many, many more who remain unlisted.

The Christian outlook on the developments that science and medicine have uncovered has been, and should continue to be, one which focuses on the benefits which innovations and improvements bring not only to the individual but to mankind as a whole. Consequently, not only are many Christians still individually contributing to the medical care of those in need in their own societies, but a huge amount of medical work in developing countries was developed and continues to be implemented through Christian commitment and activity, where there would often otherwise be little opportunity for recourse to effective healthcare.

'I've spent a number of years in India and Africa where I found much righteous endeavour undertaken by Christians of all denominations; but I never, as it happens, came across a hospital or orphanage run by the Fabian society, or a humanist leper colony.' Malcolm Muggeridge[5]

Music

The creation of music for the praise of God, but also for the expressing of the situations and emotions of daily life, has been a vital component

5 Jesus Rediscovered, New York: Pyramid 1969, 157

of Christian worship since the origin of the faith. It was medieval musicians who invented polyphony, the simultaneous sounding of two or more musical lines – permitting harmonies. It was also during this period that many instruments were perfected to develop the potential for harmonies. By the middle of the 9th Century a form of musical notation began to develop in monasteries as a mnemonic device for Gregorian chant, and in the latter part of the 10th Century an acceptable system of musical notation was invented and used commonly in order to enable music to be performed by those who had not previously heard it. Over many Centuries a massive resource of musical material was developed and with the coming of the reformation much of the music was enlivened and democratized to involve the regular congregation. Wonderfully talented composers such as the prolific Bach as well as Handel, Mendelssohn, and Brahms wrote from a reformed Christian perspective of beauty, order, joy and praise.

Engineering

An emphasis on improving the environment for the benefit of all by means of engineering and construction is in keeping with the Christian outlook of taming – or exercising dominion over – the world. Processes whereby clean water is obtained and provided, sewage is disposed of acceptably, shelter is given, bridges and safe roads are built and communication is improved are all means whereby the world is made safer and more pleasant for many. These are all fields of activity in which Christians have been involved in their instigation or implementation and have sought to observe the best principles of good stewardship; efficient use of resources, minimized environmental disruption and preference for sustainability.

And, again, Christians are frequently even now at the forefront of bringing these fundamental benefits to people in the developing world.

Measuring our days

Even the measurement of our time in the world today is dominated by the Christian cultural perspective; from the marking of our weekly calendar to the way we date history.

Effectively all the world now uses the 7 day week (which had not always been the case) and virtually everywhere takes the Sunday or Christian 'Lord's Day' as its day of rest; not only the 'Christian' West but also India and China normally observe this as their day off. Effectively only the Muslim world (generally observing Friday) or the Israeli Sabbath are exceptions.

And the world still virtually universally uses the Christian dating systems of Anno Domini – year of our Lord – and Before Christ to mark out the record of history. There are some exceptions to this also including the Islamic dating method; but the main resistance has come from secularist - humanist academics who have attempted to apply the terms CE or 'Common Era' instead of AD and BCE 'Before Common Era' instead of BC. Such an attempt at replacement nevertheless seems rather feeble in that the reference point for the beginning of the 'Common Era' is still the birth of Jesus Christ!

The avowed atheist Matthew Parris, brought up in Africa and writing in The Times, has noted that 'Christians black and white, working in Africa, do heal the sick, do teach people to read and write' – but he goes beyond this to describe how 'In Africa Christianity changes people's hearts. It brings a spiritual transformation. The rebirth is real. The change is good.'– 'The Christians were always different. Far from having cowed or confined its converts, their faith appeared to have liberated and relaxed them. There was a liveliness, a curiosity, an engagement with the world – a directness in their dealings with others...' He concluded that 'Christianity, post–Reformation and post–Luther, with its teaching of a direct, personal, two–way link between the individual and God, unmediated by the collective, and unsubordinate to any other human being......liberates'[6].

The author and screenwriter Andrew Klavan, originally from a secular Jewish background, in his autobiography – 'The Great Good Thing' – wrote about the foundational importance of Christ to Western culture; 'I was only a boy still and I didn't understand much, but I began to understand that at the heart of all Western mythology, all Western civilization, all Western writing, all Western thought, and every Western ideal, there stood a single book, the Bible, and a single man, Jesus of Nazareth. I decided I ought to find out more about them both' (Klavan 2016).

Christ is in control

In all these positive developments, successes and achievements – and for all those yet to occur – it is Christ ('in whom are hidden all the treasures of wisdom and knowledge' – Colossians 2 v 3) who has been in charge. It is He who has been displaying His authority in increasing knowledge, defeating ignorance, evil and disease and glorifying and honouring His own name in hearts and lives and culture. It is not in any strength that we or any man has that these things are achieved. Neither the burden to cultivate the power to achieve, nor the proper glory from the successes belong to us – whether or not we are otherwise weak or strong, famous or ignored. All the power and the glory is Christ's – none ours. He has built and will build His dominion until it is complete and over all to offer to the Father. Our privilege and responsibility is to be His obedient instruments; we do not have the burden of ultimate success or failure. Success is assured and it is all Christ's.

6 The Times 27/12/2008

Chapter Four

Taking back the Culture

'The relation of Christianity to culture can in many respects be seen as what we might call a secondary blessing. Most people, simply by being human, long for true humanity, for righteousness, love and goodness; if Christians are showing these things, the primary fruits of the gospel, in their lives, this will have a great influence in itself. In this way even in a sinful world – even in a world where Christians too are still far from being without sin – a 'consensus' can develop, a general cultural pattern which will include an insight into what is best and right, an understanding of what is truly human. .... even those who are living sinful lives accept the standards of the consensus.

Something like this happened in the seventeenth Century. The consensus was to a large extent the fruit of the Reformation.'

'The greatness and fullness of seventeenth-Century culture, its art and science and depth of understanding, its wealth and power, were not the result only of human endeavour – as if Christians made these things their main aim. No, they were by-products of basic Christian attitudes, and in the final analysis blessings and gifts from God. Jesus Himself told us to look first for the kingdom of God, and all these things would be given to us. And all these things, the great culture of the seventeenth Century were given after European man returned to God.' Hans Rookmaaker (Rookmaaker 1970)

So, if the pulpit were once again to take on its great foundational responsibility of building Christ's one universal kingdom throughout the world – how would it begin to bring this about?

Rookmaaker is saying that culture can change by means of a 'consensus' of its members; members who are also members of the Church; Christ's body – the practical means by which he develops and exercises his dominion.

If the body is to fulfil its role in this great enterprise the first requirement of the pulpit on this issue is to make church members aware of the reality of Christ's One Kingdom, His irresistible intention to bring it about and their privilege and responsibility in its accomplishment. They must be aware of the plan, its inevitable success and their role - small or large – in it.

So, the first thing the pastorate must do is to preach a different vision; positive, outgoing, optimistic – but also costly, sustained, long–term and inevitably confrontational. Unless the people see the vision and destination they will not know where to go and will have no hope of achieving it. This must be the Church's expression of a divinely ordained 'Tiocfaidh ar la'[7]!

In addition, however, once the strategic long-term overview has been articulated, the pulpit needs to guide its members, Christ's body, into the specific elements which are within their remits and which will begin to effect cultural transformation.

One way of outlining the areas of responsibility of individual Christians is to consider the various forms of government which God has put in place; Church government, family government, civil government and

7 Irish for 'Our day will come'

self–government. For the individual Christian it is family government and self-government which are most relevant; but these can have huge ramifications within a culture – 'the home is the molecule which builds every larger culture' (D. J. Wilson 1998) – so spinning organically out of these two are two more huge areas of cultural power; Education and Business.

Family

The believer's family should be based on the foundational creational picture described in Genesis where the husband is the head over the wife and family. Husband and wife are together undertaking again the task of the Cultural Mandate and the husband is the head and leader in this enterprise. So in whatever way the family is involved in extending Christ's kingdom; whether through profession, occupation, business, education or otherwise, the husband should be initiating and leading the way and the wife supporting. This is also the picture portrayed in the relationship between Christ and His Church in Ephesians Chapter 5. Because the requirement for leadership extends out into the nitty–gritty of the texture of the tough outside world and its many difficult people, situations and practicalities, this will need husbands to develop and expand their 'savoir faire' – their skills and qualities in these areas. It will mean that their role as head and leader will extend greatly beyond the thin tokenistic observation of the principle of male headship often characterized by a lack of thorough participation in the real world.

Of course, the headship required should also be a loving and sacrificial one as again exemplified by Christ's pattern in Ephesians Chapter 5.

Education

The mandate for involvement of believers in the vital sphere of education also begins in the family; fathers are directed to bring up their children in the training and admonition of the Lord (Ephesians 6 v 4), and we are reminded in Proverbs 22 v 6 to 'Train a child in the way he should go, and when he is old he will not turn from it'; knowledge and principles which are learnt as a child are the foundation of our character and behaviour as adults.

Of course, the question arises; what is the 'training and admonition of the Lord'? Is this confined to the understanding of morality, teaching about God, Christ and salvation etc.; the religious and spiritual aspects of life? If so, it can be safely left to family worship and discussion, and to teaching in Sunday School or church. And this approach fits with the currently prevailing view that these are the only areas which are within Christ's kingdom and which are the primary concern of believers. If, however, the dominion of the Lord extends to all aspects of culture and creation – then these too are within the ambit of necessary training and admonition, and must be addressed and supervised by the father if he is to equip his children in their future role as part of Christ's body in extending His Kingdom.

Parents may consider that the 'ordinary' subjects of school; History, Geography, Literature and Science, are 'neutral' and that these subjects can be safely taught in a secular environment – leaving the issues of faith, morality, values and meaning to be addressed at home or Sunday School. But if Christ is King over all there is no neutrality, and by addressing children's education in this fragmented way we are obscuring His overall centrality and dominion. As Cornelius van Til has said; 'Every fact in this world, the God of the Bible claims, has His stamp indelibly engraved upon it'[8].

8 Why I believe in God. Philadelphia: Committee on Christian Education, Orthodox Presbyterian Church, n.d.

If this is correct, then all these subjects – including mathematics and English – must be addressed and taught from a Christian perspective. If not, they will be taught from a sinful, secular perspective; not a 'neutral' one – and this is what we are seeing progressively in the state school system. This involves, not just specific scientific theories such as evolution or revision of ethical practices such as sexual morality, but the foundational principles underlying and intertwined with modern teaching.

So, what sorts of faulty principles are ingrained in modern secular teaching? The first might be the idea of Student Centred Learning. This can reinforce in the student that they are the centre; the most important, and this notion is likely to be carried on throughout their student career and future life. It is surely antithetical to the Christian approach; which, while not denying the significance of the individual, should centre on God and give great consideration for others and legitimate respect to the authority of parents and teachers.

Another concept widely adopted in modern secular education is Rousseau's idea of the 'noble savage'. Rousseau, whom C.S. Lewis has dubbed 'the father of the totalitarians'[9], taught that man in his youth is uncorrupted and that his perfect nature is corrupted by society. He believed that children are born into a morally neutral 'state of nature' which can be directed by education to goodness. This pernicious notion runs completely contrary to Christian belief in man's innate corrupted and sinful nature. It is also a licence to attempt to manipulate the blank slate of children's minds to construct a new society in the likeness of the progressive and secular teachers and leaders.

---

9 'On the transmission of Christianity', 1946: essay in 'God in the Dock'

In terms of human rights teaching; there is a correct and legitimate understanding of human rights whereby our rights are matched with corresponding obligations; where the right to life implies an obligation on others not to take our life, rights to equality before the law and an assumption of innocence until proven guilty require an obligation on the legal system to honour these points. Many of these reasonable rights have their foundation in biblical and Christian principles and are worthy of respect. However, the range of so–called rights now extends to include, among others, a right to affordable housing, a right to a job, a right to education, a right for children to play and a right to a nationality – none of which have an evident appropriate party to which the obligation should be attached. Further, the scope of categories and 'identities' to which these protections apply continues to expand. Teaching regarding human rights has become thoroughly integrated into the secular education system from primary school onwards and their status has become elevated beyond virtually any other moral or practical consideration. Consequently, for students who are products of these schools, observation of these rights has become an inviolable imperative above all others, including any conflicting Biblical guidance.

In addition to the educational ambience created by the background features described above the specific subjects taught will have greatly differing perspectives depending on whether they are regarded from a secular or a Christian perspective.

Take history for example, is it a narrative of inevitable positive progress occurring in an environment of fluid and developing morality, as some secularists might see it – or is it as Christians should see it; full of meaning, with a purpose, a beginning and an end, set in a context of good and evil and with an overseeing omnipotent God? These are not trivial considerations.

With geography, is the structure of the world determined by the actions of God or by blind uniformitarian processes? How is man's position regarding the environment to be seen? Are resources deterministic of national or individual economic success or are there other factors in play?

Literature is full of situations and dilemmas where a range of different moral values and considerations may apply. Which are to be promoted and honoured and which are to be despised? Is there an objective morality? Is there absolute truth? Does the secularist decide or does the Christian decide?

Economics and politics raise questions of property and ownership and ideas of fairness. Are these all going to be 'neutral'?
Each area requires its own specific detailed review and consideration but all these subjects and more, including mathematics and physics, can be regarded, analyzed and taught from a Christian perspective in contrast to the prevailing secularism. Christian parents are failing in their God given responsibility if they carelessly throw their children into the lions' den of secular education. The consequences can be profound; 70% of church going young people who attend state colleges in the US have given up on their faith by the time they finish their degree.

Whether parents choose to educate children at home or to send them to Christian schools is for their careful consideration. Either of these options are likely to have significant financial and other implications – but the implications of providing the right education for their children's characters, values and skills will have an immense impact on whether they are likely to become compliant conformists in the empire of progressive orthodoxy, or godly, self–governing Kingdom culture builders.

A proper commitment to Christian education must logically extend to involvement beyond primary and secondary level to University or College level, because it is in this environment that many of the powerful new cultural concepts and trends are generated and propagated – eight out of ten British academics are left wing[10] – permeating out through the media, government and other professions as graduates progress. Obviously it will be demanding to initially found and staff any such institutions and there will be particular problems in obtaining accreditation and funding; many Christian higher education establishments in the United States which have received state funding are now greatly vulnerable to pressure to conform to the implementation of authoritarian policies regarding the pervasive new moral imperatives. 'He who pays the piper calls the tune'!

Concerns regarding funding extend beyond the institutions to the individual students; most students in the UK are now leaving their colleges and universities many thousands of pounds in debt – essentially to the government. At present the repayment regime seems to be relatively benign, but the student debtors are surely critically vulnerable to potential future coercive pressure to conform to, for instance, government-imposed policies when applying for or obtaining employment. Remembering Proverbs 22 v 7, that 'the borrower is servant to the lender', they and their parents need to be wary of making themselves vulnerable by this debt burden to malign pressure to compromise with godless practices.

10 Lackademia: Why do academics lean left? 2017, Adam Smith Institute

Self

The responsibility of self–government under God applies to every mature person; he or she must give individual account to God for all his or her actions or inactions in every sphere. He cannot abdicate his personal decisions and responsibilities by surrendering them to some other authority such as a church, a state, a tribe or family or a business; and for the Christian in particular it is clear that there is no mediator between God and man except Jesus Christ.

So, what does such self-government consist of? It requires both the functions of moral and intellectual discernment; we must train ourselves to be able to evaluate, discern and decide regarding the intertwining practical and moral aspects of every type of issue. The mature man must not only be capable of making correct moral judgements but must develop up his knowledge and understanding of many other matters so that he is able to exercise his own judgment rather than being 'led by the nose' by others seeking to influence him; more than that, self–government means having the confidence and courage to act in keeping with his own judgment. So self–government involves the input of both the moral and intellectual capabilities. Not only must we exercise this ability in our addressing, evaluating and deciding on outside issues which we face – but we also must exercise government over ourselves; self-control – constraining and restraining our own behaviours and desires.

So, what sort of outcomes might we expect to see when mature individuals are able to act with wise self–governance? Proper use of discernment and judgment over a whole range of issues will result; from more informed opinions about scientific or political controversies such as global warming, sustainability or Brexit, more competent evaluation of legal issues such as guilt and innocence, proper justice and proportionate penalties, to careful and better consideration of Church teaching and the content of sermons.

The ability to be more critical of media output, from current affairs programmes to films and soaps should become more apparent. The discerning self–governing individual will be immune to the hysteria of rabble-rousing radio hosts, will seek to hear all the facts before jumping to conclusions and will be resistant to climbing onto any kind of bandwagon or joining any kind of lynch mob. He will not be easy fodder for any form of media manipulation or demagoguery, whether political or theological, and Christian self–government will be evident in a host of other apparently lesser contexts; as a student, an employee, a citizen or neighbour. In each of these situations by exercising independent Christ honouring thought and ethical and courageous action individual Christians can be the gritty salt affecting the nooks and crannies of many corners of the culture.

Christian self–government is the foundation for the other three main forms of government instituted by God; Church government, family government and civil government. The man properly armed with the ability of self–government will not be amenable to domination or manipulation under any of the other forms of government and will be suitably equipped to participate and exercise authority in them when opportunity arises or duty calls.

Business

We must remember that Adam was a gardener and Jesus was a carpenter, and it would be difficult to overestimate the potential for businesses to affect individual lives, change the culture and build the kingdom; through employment, their internal culture and practices, their interaction with their customers and suppliers, and the nature and quality of the products and services which they provide.

A business is a small (or large) kingdom and culture in its own right where the owner or proprietor can legitimately exercise constructive and creative godly authority over the area under his control. It is a specific sphere where he can assert Christ's dominion over this part of 'the garden'.

Such enterprises shouldn't be developed as 'business minus' i.e. business minus Sunday working, corrupt practices, financial dishonesty or greed, but instead as 'business plus' i.e. businesses which treat their employees fairly, provide top quality products and services – desiring to serve others, and act fairly and proportionally with justice and mercy, showing beauty not only in what they provide but how they provide it. Their activities will also generate prosperity which will also be evident through legitimate corporate and individual tax revenues.

And when we consider businesses such as farms, supermarkets, mines, boiler makers, taxi drivers, truck drivers, plumbers and every other legitimate form of commercial activity we must remember that these are all the mechanisms by which God provides for the needs of 'our daily bread'. The things they provide are essential for serving their brothers and sisters and all their neighbours and fellow men. And in conducting business fairly over a period of time when beef or parsnips, domestic decorating, dentistry or podiatry are provided, the proprietor must be working in a relationship with his customer which is not one of exploitation but of respect, compromise and give and take. The business owner himself will also be in a similar such relationship with his raw material suppliers, his solicitors, accountants and IT providers.

These are real contacts between the day to day lives of those on either side of any business transaction and, if conducted with consistency and integrity, provide a background framework against which the sincerity and reality of any 'Gospel' message can be fairly judged.
Undertaking a business enterprise requires not only a desire to build the Kingdom in this way, but the cultivation of the skills to carry it out effectively. These will vary hugely from business to business, but require great depth and breadth of knowledge of the world in all its aspects from; the laws of nature, characteristics of the elements and of specific materials, understanding of communication and human personality as well as specific areas of knowledge such as accountancy, languages, law, medicine, history and geography. An effective businessman must know a huge amount about the real world as a whole as well as having a deep, thorough and growing understanding of his own specific area of expertise. In other words, a man grounded in the world, as well as of the Spirit.

To carry out this endeavour properly, we need to always be aware of the fundamental element of service to others inherent in his work. Kingdom businesses must not only be successful and profitable but also be serving their neighbour.

And it is vital and practical to remember that successful and righteous businesses will not only provide a credible platform for a gospel witness to their customers and suppliers but may through the giving of their owners and employees provide financial support for church institutions, gospel preaching and missionary activity. In fact, such giving is an inherent component of sustaining the church, and a pulpit which fails to legitimize the Kingdom calling to business may in due course lead to the withering away of the more 'religious' aspects of Kingdom activity.

We often hear inducements from preachers to listen to God's voice where He may be calling us from our work as a teacher, civil servant, salesman or financier to train for the ministry or go to the mission field, but would we ever contemplate calling someone from the mission field or even from the ministry to enter a job in 'the City' or in some other business occupation? Is it not possible that God could call in this way? Why not?

The call is more important than the calling; 'If a man goes to the mission field in disobedience, he is being unholy in it. And if a man becomes a rancher in obedience then he is being holy in it' (D. Wilson 2019).

Civil government

The three great spheres of authority are the Church, the family and the state; and Christ has dominion over all three. Believers must be guided as to a right understanding of the correct but limited role of the state in this triad in order to play their part in engaging with its proper activities and resisting its improper intrusions; such engagement or resistance will require the righteous capacity for self–government as already described.

The activities of the state should be limited; the maintenance of external and internal security, the provision of justice, sufficient regulation to promote the harmonious interaction of the citizens and the collection of the necessary amount of taxes to carry out these activities.

The state should not become the provider of an increasingly extensive range of our requirements; it should not be regarded as our saviour – it should never become our God. Unfortunately, the modern secular state is inclining to do these things more and more, and most Christians have been happy to let it do so. But not only should it never be regarded as our saviour – it, of course, can never succeed in that objective and will only ever disappoint. The other overweening tendency of the modern state is to regulate and control – moving towards a tyranny over its citizens. Christians must resist this; we must not become 'slaves of men' (1 Cor 7 v 23).

Of course, there are many ways in which Christians should be legitimately involved and supportive of the state either in some form of official position or employment ranging from local councillor to MP, or from police officer to civil servant and tax collector. Or simply as a citizen finding themselves in direct contact with any of these.

All who are officers or employees of the state or its subsidiaries are effectively in civil magistrate (or lesser magistrate) roles, and, of course, very much of what they are required to do will be entirely legitimate and necessary. And, in course of time – as the Christian consensus revives and extends, they may find themselves in the forefront of remodeling and shaping the apparatus of society to more practically express Christ's dominion. Ultimately, however, in all these positions we are under the authority of Christ, and because of this Christians in these roles must be prepared to disobey those in immediate authority above them when God's law is being flouted. We all must remember that 'the king must never be above the Law' (Deuteronomy 17 v 18–20).

Similarly, as ordinary citizens we must be very content and amenable to comply with all proper and legitimate regulation and enforcement by the state but must also be prepared to resist and refuse when necessary. It is in these very testing and stressful situations when the abilities of the Christian to judge wisely and well, with good understanding and to act with courage will be required. When this happens it will be very necessary for the officers of the church to stand with their members and fellow believers rather than shy away from conflict with the state.

Because these situations will arise increasingly, it is necessary that believers prepare themselve to face shame or embarrassment or indeed unemployment or incarceration at virtually any time. This is a further reminder for Christians to avoid the burden of debt which increases their vulnerability to compromise when under pressure.

Everything else

Christians' freedom and individual circumstances mean that they can and should be open to be involved in any area or human activity which is not forbidden to them, and although the foundational elements of extending out Christ's kingdom are primarily through the family and education there are very many other mechanisms and disciplines which are crucial to the delivery and permeation of ideas and principles into all the nooks and crannies of culture. Many of these areas can reasonably be considered under the following outline categories; communication media, art, music and literature and material culture

Communication Media

'I meet people occasionally who think motion pictures, the product Hollywood makes, is merely entertainment, has nothing to do with education. That's one of the darndest fool fallacies... Anything that brings you to tears by way of drama does something to the deepest roots of our personality. All movies, good or bad, are educational and Hollywood is the foremost educational institution on earth.' Carl Sandburg[11]

'The Media' are the whole multifarious range of channels for the communication of information, some old, some very new; radio, television, newspapers, news channels, film, social media, streaming services, podcasts and more. Although there are now an almost

11 US Information Agency News Release No. SR-818-614, 1964

unlimited number of sub-channels, in some of these categories there are very strongly dominant brands such as the BBC, CNN, Fox or the Huffington Post, and receivers of all this information only have so much 'head–space' to acknowledge and accept a limited number of brands or to absorb the specific communications. This leaves those in control of these sources having tremendous power and influence; in virtually every instance the material passing along the channel will be edited – many topics will not even be considered for publication by those in charge.

And none of this selection or editing will be neutral; everything comes from a point of view – conscious or unconscious; and nearly all of it will be conscious. Very many of those who work in the media (whether producers, scriptwriters, editors or presenters) will have strong commitments to causes or agenda which are antipathetic to the Gospel. Even the apparently inconsequential 'soaps' or dramas are far from innocuous, in bringing current controversial issues into their storyline they are often treating topics such as homosexuality or transgenderism in such a way as to render them acceptable as 'real–life' situations.

The mature self–governing Christian must always be aware that there is no neutrality in the media and must learn to critically assess the material he is exposed to. In addition to this in this hugely powerful cultural sphere Christians need to see its strategic importance in propagating ideas and principles and must be ready to make themselves available to God's call to work in any of the roles described above for which he has equipped them. In particular those who find themselves involved in news or current affairs disciplines will have the responsibility and privilege of telling the truth, in contrast to the devil's trade in lies.

Art, Music and Literature

'All art is propaganda' George Orwell[12]

We are reminded again that nothing is neutral – everything comes from a point of view. And we can see in many of the forms of visual art that the images portrayed are often of confusion, discordance or meaninglessness, in keeping with a world without God. Literature also often reflects this. All of these aspects of art (particularly music) also often are designed to entertain, and entertainment itself is not necessarily bad; it helps us relax and recreate, see things from a different aspect and share in it with others. Music, too, provides a diverse way of interacting with our emotions – reflecting or stimulating joy, sadness, danger or confidence; able to unite people together.

All these forms of art are almost inevitable expressions of our God-given creativity; to be expected because we are created in the image of the original Creator. However, unlike Him, we can only create within the parameters he has set us.

So, if we are to extend Christ's kingdom through these inescapable features which provide such rich backdrop to all our lives, how should we do it?

Those who are gifted or desiring to follow these paths must apply themselves to developing their competence and skills in order to be able to carry out their work with excellence, and they must then express it in a true, honourable and beautiful way. In doing so they not only are serving Christ, but also blessing and serving their neighbours.

12 Critical Essays, 1941

Material Culture - 'Architecture and Morality'

'See I have chosen Bezalel son of Uri, the son of Hur, of the tribe of Judah, and I have filled him with the Spirit of God, with skill, ability and knowledge in all kinds of crafts – to make artistic designs for work in gold, silver and bronze, to cut and set stones, to work in wood, and to engage in all kinds of craftsmanship...' Exodus 31 v 2–5

Material culture is all the tangible, practical things that people make - buildings, cars, door frames, door handles, fabrics, clothing, furniture, cutlery, mobile phones and everything else.

In all these things the ideas and beliefs of the designers and manufacturers are expressed including, for example, the post–war 'Brutalist' architecture influenced by Marxism whose constructions are still around us. But it is not only the structure of these material items which is relevant; they are also very often embellished with colour, patterns and textures which can also reflect underlying ideas. All these things are so prevalent and pervasive that we are usually only barely aware of them – but they are of huge significance in our lives.

The shape of buildings where we meet or work, or which are our homes affect our mood and our effectiveness. The nature and design of the fabrics which we wear or which adorn our homes are also significant in influencing us, and all of these things can be expressions – however thinly – of the underlying ideas which they may gently propagate.

So, once again, we need to be aware of the influence of these things on us, and of the legitimacy and potential for our own involvement in these areas in order to express Christ's Kingdom and its values as well as serving our neighbours through beautiful and effective products.

'If an endless field of human knowledge and of human ability is now being formed by all that takes place in order to make the visible world and material culture subject to us, and if we know that this dominion of ours over nature will be complete in eternity, we may conclude that the knowledge and dominion we have gained over nature here can and will be of continued significance, even in the kingdom of glory.' Abraham Kuyper

Chapter Five

Conclusion

Everybody wants to change the world; the socialists, the feminists, the nationalists, the Moslems, Jeff Bezos, Bill Gates, Elon Musk, Google etc. Everybody but those who have a mandate, an instruction and the power to do so!

At the centre of the issues that have been discussed are two deeply contrasting views of Christ's Kingdom and of the role and message of the Church. At the heart of the prevalent view in the mainstream evangelical and reformed church today is, and has been for many years, a truncated view of the Kingdom and the Gospel; the borders of Christ's Kingdom are seen as circumscribing the Church, evangelistic and missionary activities, and our personal spiritual lives. Everything outside these bounds is worldly, of little true significance for us, and is not something we are able, or even should try, to influence or change; and although Christ may be King there in some form, it is not for us to be concerned or involved. It is a message shorn of the cultural mandate. The Gospel itself is of course essential for the personal spiritual benefit of all who believe, but there is no good news for the culture, creation or the world as a whole.

The alternative view sees Christ's kingdom as being undivided; he is as much king over the kings and nations of the earth as he is king over our hearts as well as over every aspect of geography, history, science, arts and culture. And the church and his people are the means whereby that underlying authority is to be made extant. As Kuyper has memorably said; 'There is not a square inch in the whole domain of our human existence over which Christ, who is sovereign over all, does not cry, Mine!'. There is no implication in this view that evangelism or personal spiritual growth should be compromised or impaired – the culture is not to be prioritized over the Gospel. There is no conflict between the two. The dominant current limited view of Christ's kingdom, however, with its abandonment of the cultural mandate has resulted in hugely distorting effects on the culture, the practical and spiritual life of the individual believer, and of the church itself.

When the culture is no longer of significance to believers, they retreat from, or only pay lacklustre attention to, its issues; the arts, science, media and law are impoverished of the salt of Christian influence or godly structuring. Education becomes a free–for–all for sinful, secular notions; contaminating generations to come with false ideas. The family is prey to humanistic, pseudo–scientific ways of operating, and business inclines more to greed and corruption, producing products and services bereft of Christian input and pandering obsequiously to the fluctuating trends of a morally rootless culture.

Christian individuals fail to cultivate their practical knowledge of the world and the general skills to live in it effectively, as well as developing less comprehensive knowledge of the specific skills and competences of their own occupation or profession. They have less involvement or competence in the practical and political affairs of their community, again leaving these matters in the hands of those with less edifying agendas. The facility for self–government will also decline – not being much required for a man who is not engaging with the world – and this will mean that the individual is less able to constructively assess, or challenge, the output of the pulpit or session. Without any great significance for Christ or his rule in their lives, believers and their businesses will tend to conform to the patterns of the world.

The remaining roles of the church can also be deprived by a lack of practical engagement of business or individuals with unbelievers, such that the integrity of their witness to the gospel message is not vindicated for its practical reality, and, of course, to some extent, lack of success in the financial sphere will lead to declining tithes and offerings for the regular work of the church.

The church itself has tended to become distorted by its dismissal of the significance of cultural matters to its calling and its corresponding concentration on 'things above'. As the other forms of government instituted by God, such as state, family and self, fade away in importance, so the church itself and its activities, along with certain evangelistic endeavours, assume an unbalanced importance in the lives of individual believers. Power and influence tend to move towards the elders and indeed the pastor, and away from the individual believer. At the same time, however, observation of some of the injunctions of Scripture regarding, for instance, the roles of men and women, become thinner and more tokenistic – having lost their hinterland of relevance in the culture as a whole.

If culture is religion externalized, then the reason we have declining Christian culture is because evangelicals keep their religion internalized – and current evangelicalism is increasingly focused on the church and its activities – retreating from the world. It has a defensive 'circling the wagons' mentality. The trouble with this approach is that it is doomed to fail; 'If the Church is not transforming the culture around her, then the culture around her is transforming the Church' (D. Wilson 2016). It is a bit like Northern Ireland playing Brazil in a soccer match, with the Northern Ireland team adopting a strategy of having a team of defenders with '11 men behind the ball' – they can never win. And if they don't concede a goal in normal time, or even in extra time, they certainly won't win the penalty shoot–out!

So, the church and its leaders must turn their backs on this policy of abdication and defeatism, resuming their obedience to the one King over all, and to their obligation as his servants and instruments as he makes his kingdom evident in every aspect of the world and culture.

Such a more full–blooded approach will inevitably result in confrontation and resistance from the hegemony of secularism in many, many situations leading to shame and embarrassment, perhaps loss of livelihood and freedoms – even to physical harm.

Therefore, the pastors, elders and believers generally, need to be prepared for combat and to develop courage; they need to be prepared to experience defeat, to suffer reversals and perhaps be casualties themselves – the Christian virtue of courage needs to be restored.

And ultimately it will be the gospel that needs to be preached – the full unrestricted gospel which glorifies Christ above all and is good news for every man and woman and for the whole world.

Epilogue

As Father Mapple's sermon in the Whaleman's Chapel drew to a close, and having given his main lesson to the congregation; 'Sin not; but if you do, take heed to repent of it like Jonah', he gave a second to himself as a 'prophet–pilot' of the pulpit;

'This, shipmates, this is that other lesson; and woe to that pilot of the living God who slights it. Woe to him whom this world charms from gospel duty! Woe to him who seeks to pour oil upon the waters when God has brewed them into a gale! Woe to him who seeks to please rather than to appal! Woe to him whose good name is more to him than goodness! Woe to him who, in this world, courts not dishonor! Woe to him who would not be true, even though to be false were salvation! Yea, woe to him who, as the great Pilot Paul has it, while preaching to others is himself a castaway!'

Appendix 1

Babylon? - The only form of exile is self–exile

A very prevalent recent metaphor for describing the Church's current situation is to say that we are in exile in Babylon. This has been promoted in a number of recent books such as Rod Dreher's 'The Benedict Option', James Thompson's 'The Church in Exile: God's Counterculture in a Non–Christian World, and Lee Beach's 'The Church in Exile: Living in Hope After Christendom'. It has also featured in multiple sermons, seminars and articles including, prominently, Carl Trueman's 'A Church for Exiles'.

So, how is this appealingly 'scriptural' analogy being applied to the Church in our time? Proponents of this idea see the church as being forced into an 'internal exile', within the culture which we had helped to form and where we previously were strongly influential. The secular culture sees the church as being at best irrelevant and often as malign, and is increasingly intolerant of its beliefs, values and morals. This, of course, is not (for the present) a physical exile – but is an exile from the world of ideas and from the actions which would flow from them. It amounts to the loss of any significant role in the public square and involves increasing scrutiny and constraint from the authorities. The adoption of the exile idea is an acceptance of its reality and validity as the correct paradigm for the church's current status in the world. And it's important, because like any such powerful metaphor, it will significantly direct how we think and behave under its influence.

But how valid is this description? How well does it compare to the biblical Babylonian exile which it seeks to parallel?

Due to the repeated sinfulness, corruption, disobedience and idolatry of the Jewish people, God warned and prophesied to them through Jeremiah that Jerusalem would be destroyed by the Babylonians and that many of the people would be carried off to exile in that land. He also prophesied through Jeremiah, however, that after 70 years of exile He would end their exile and bring them back to their own country and would bless their future. So, in the historical narrative we have an all-powerful God who clearly warns through prophetic words that He will judge and punish his people for their specific sins by exiling them for a specific time. We also realize that this exile not only has the function of punishing the people, but also of purifying them and consolidating their practices.

Where, then, are the parallels for today? Has God delivered such a judgement? For what sins? Who was the prophet? When did he speak? Does the exile have an expected end? No, none of these questions are answered – none of these features are evident and there is no reason to believe that God has ordained any such exile.

If the omnipotent God has not authorized the exile of the church, who has? The kingdoms of the world; the secular empire? There is no authority which has any such right to pronounce such a judgement on God's people. There is only one legitimate Emperor who can exercise such authority and dominion and that is Christ himself. If Christ has not exiled us, then we are not exiled!

And there is only one mechanism whereby this faux exile can come to pass, and that is by accepting and complying with this false notion so often propagated in these days – and exiling ourselves. To adopt such a course of action would, of course, be flagrant disobedience and abdication of our role and calling as the means whereby Christ's dominion is developed and exercised in the world. The Church is not passive flotsam in the turmoil of the world's arbitrary currents or stranded and waiting high and dry until the return of a future benevolent tide releases us. No, Christ rules overall and His people are His instruments for change. They have the power to make the cultural climate.

The reason why we appear to be 'exiled' or irrelevant is not something that 'has just happened to us' – it is something we are responsible for. The attitudes which validate the Babylonian fallacy are the ones which have brought about its plausibility; denial of Christ's power and authority, defeatism, retreat from the world, cowardice and compliance. Consequently, despite Carl Trueman's 'We do not expect to be at the center of worldly affairs. We do not imagine ourselves to be running indispensable institutions...' and 'We expect cultural exile. It actually confirms our deepest convictions about the way the world is.' (Trueman 2014) and for all its attractiveness as a historical scriptural paradigm, this analogy should be junked by all believers who properly honour the sovereignty of Christ.

If we are in exile, we are there voluntarily, and if voluntarily, then we will have been culpable in orchestrating our own irrelevance and ineffectiveness and will have only ourselves to blame.

Appendix 2

Key takeaway points

- The pulpit has the power to change the world
- Christ's resurrection power is available and necessary for us in all our endeavours – not only those in or around the church
- The pulpit needs to proclaim Christ's dominion and authority and the positive message that his plan and promise to conquer all is assured, and that every Christian has a role in the successful conquest
- The pulpit needs to preach that this is a long term and costly commitment
- The pulpit needs to teach the importance of the godly institution of the family and of the husband's role in leading it
- Believers need to develop their competence in the skills required in the practicalities of the world around them and in particular the skills required in their own specific callings
- The pulpit needs to emphasize the importance and responsibility of parents for the godly education of their children, and to warn against the dangers of leaving their children in the hands of the secularists
- The pulpit needs to inculcate in believers an awareness of the importance of self–government; to be able to judge wisely, take responsibility and make decisions
- Believers must never rush to judgement of a person or an issue, especially not to follow the crowd to do so. They must always allow the person to explain their side of the story and never convict without solid and reliable evidence

- Work on the wider Kingdom will often be in service to our neighbour
- Believers and Christian organizations should try to avoid debt as much as possible – especially indebtedness to the government. This includes student loans
- Be prepared to go to wherever God calls – whether to the mission field or the milking parlour. It is God's prerogative to appoint, our responsibility to obey
- As 'lesser magistrates' Christians must be ready to obey God's law within their remit; if necessary, in defiance of higher authority
- Be ready every day to be fired from your job, or to walk away from it; if obedience to God requires it

The LORD has surely given the whole land into our hands... (Joshua 2 v 24)

References

Aikman, David. 2003. Jesus in Beijing. Washington, DC: Regnery Publishing.

Hawking, Stephen. 2006. God created the integers. London: Penguin Books.

Kelly, Douglas F. 1992. The emergence of liberty in the modern world: the influence of Calvin on five governments from the 16th though 18th centuries. Phillipsburg: Presbyterian and Reformed Publishing Company.

Klavan, Andrew. 2016. The Great Good Thing: A Secular Jew comes to Faith in Christ. Nashville: Thomas Nelson.

Mangalwadi, Vishal. 2011. The book that made your world. Nashville: Thomas Nelson.

Needham, Joseph. 1954–1984. Science and Civilization in China. Cambridge: Cambridge University Press.

Rookmaaker, H.R. 1970. Modern Art and the Death of a Culture. London: Inter-Varsity Press.

Schaeffer, Francis A. 1974. No Little People. Downers Grove: InterVarsity Press.

Stark, R. 2005. The Victory of Reason: how Christianity led to freedom, capitalism, and Western success. New York: Random House Trade Paperbacks.

Trueman, Carl. 2014. "A Church for Exiles." First Things.

Whitehead, Alfred North. 1967. Science and the Modern World. New York: The Free Press.

Wilson, D. 2016. Empires of Dirt: Secularism, Radical Islam, and the Mere Christendom Alternative. Moscow, ID: Canon Press and Book Service.

Wilson, D Jones and D. 1998. Angels in the Architecture: A Protestant Vision for Middle Earth. Moscow, ID: Canon Press and Book Service.

Wilson, Douglas. 2019. dougwils.com. Accessed June 13, 2020.